To

_____

From

_____

Date

_____

MYSTERIES OF

TATTOOING

AND THE POWER OF

PURITY

THE
CORNERSTONE
PUBLISHING

GLORY OLUCHI IKEORA

Mysteries of Tattooing and the Power of Purity

Published by:
Cornerstone Publishing
A Division of Cornerstone Creativity Group LLC
Info@thecornerstonepublishers.com
www.thecornerstonepublishers.com
516.547.4999

Author's Contact

For booking to speak at your next event or to order bulk copies of this book please use information below:

Phone: +1 (510) 690-7832

Email: Olukama1@gmail.com

DEDICATION

This book is dedicated to God, and to all men and women doing exploit in the Kingdom of God.

CONTENTS

Dedication..5

Chapter 1
The Mysteries And Dangers of Tattooing.......9

Chapter 2
The Vices Of Tattooing................................19

Chapter 3
The Way Out..37

PART 2: PURITY

Chapter 1
What Is Purity?..49

Chapter 2
Classification of Purity.................................55

Chapter 3
What The Heart of A Child of God is Meant
For...71

Chapter 4

Purity in The Place of Worship....................79

About The Author

Chapter 1

THE MYSTERIES OF TATTOOING

Tattooing is abomination before God because it is a perversion of His word. The Bible condemns the act of tattooing. The Nelson's dictionary of the Bible defines Tattoo as a permanent mark or design fixed upon the body by a process of pricking the skin and inserting an indelible color under the skin. The moral and ceremonial laws of Leviticus forbids this practice. Therefore, any kind of self-laceration or marking of the body was prohibited among the Hebrew people. Such cuttings were associated with pagan cults that tattooed their followers while they mourned the dead.

The Bible is God's word to man and the final

authority on how we are to live and conduct our daily lives. These are perilous times, with an increase in worldliness, carnality and rebellion to God's authority. The current day fashion trend clearly goes against the Word of God. There is a craze to pursue worldliness and justify disobedience to God and to His Word by using changing fashion trends as an excuse.

The Lord clearly condemns tattooing and hates it with perfect hatred because it is the perversion of His word.

"Ye shall not make any cutting in your flesh for the dead nor print any mark upon you. I am the Lord" (Leviticus 19:28)

Any incision or mark done on the body to justify a fashion trend or initiation is carnal, and any form of carnality is sin.

"Because the carnal mind is enmity against God; for it is not subject to the law of God, neither indeed can be" (Romans 8:7).

One of the reasons why God condemned Tattoo and forbids Israel from participating in it was because it was an ancient culture practiced by heathen nations in honor of the dead as a pagan ceremonial act of mourning.

Although some Christians believe that tatto is the same with getting a haircut, I insist that tatto is a pagan practice. Believe it or not . . . this is a widely used argument.

Leviticus 19:26-28 is a clear condemnation of pagan, witchcraft and heathen practices. Look at the context. Verse 26 is plainly referring to "enchantment [spells or witchcraft] nor observe times [astrology]...Verse 28 is the pagan, demonic practice of bloodletting [cuttings in your flesh] and tattooing. Why would the Lord stick in the middle a verse that "condemns simply getting a haircut"? Of course, He wouldn't. . . And He didn't. . .

Leviticus 19:26-28 reads:

26 Ye shall not eat any thing with the blood: neither shall ye use enchantment, nor observe times. 27 Ye shall not round the corners of your heads, neither shalt thou mar the corners of thy beard. 28 Ye shall not make any cuttings in your flesh for the dead, nor print any marks upon you: I am the LORD.

The condemnation found in verse 27 of "rounding the corners of your head" or "mar the corners of thy beard" was the forbidding of a common pagan practice that cut the hair as worship and honor of the hosts of heaven (Terry Watkins).

Tattoo was used in some eras to mark and identify slaves and criminals, as a result dehumanizing the individual. It is also associated with gangsters and convicts; therefore, it could be identified as an indecent appearance as a result of which some corporations require that their staff wear clothes that would cover any form of tattoo. It is a mark of perversion, which comprises homosexuality, lesbianism, bisexuality, fetishism, mania and many bipolar disorders. A religious leader in Ghana "Mallan Ya Wadudu clearly warned against the harmful effect of tattoos, he said that it can cause homosexuality and prostitution, stating that the snake, scorpion and frogs and other animal symbols they put on themselves all have spiritual meaning.

One may say that tattoo is now an acceptable fashion and it is worn by celebrities. But a close look at anybody wearing it reveals one social disorder or another. According to Kate Devlin in April 2009 wrote that tattoo is associated with low self-esteem. Also "the journal of criminal law, criminology and police science in 1968 by Northwest university school of Law written by Richard S. Post stated that tattoo or any form of body marking can serve to indicate the presence of a personality disorder which could or is characterized by behaviors which deviates from contemporary social norms.

Tattooing is a sign of apostasy and it always poses danger to those who bear it.

2 Peter 2:20-22

"For if after they have escaped the pollutions of the world through the knowledge of the Lord and Saviour Jesus Christ, they are again entangled therein, and overcome, the latter end is worse with them than the beginning. For it had been better for them not to have known the way of righteousness, than, after they have known it, to turn from the holy commandment delivered unto them. But it is happened unto them according to the true proverb, The dog is turned to his own vomit again; and the sow that was washed to her wallowing in the mire."

Titus1:16

"They profess that they know God; but in works they deny him, being abominable, and disobedient, and unto

every good work reprobate."

Since tattooing is also a form of art, the design could be in the form of flowers, figures, leaves, stars, names, animals and fanciful devices on various parts of the body. Some even mark the names of their dead loved ones on their bodies. Marking the names of the dead on the body is a mark of idolatry. In the ancient days, the tattooist made use of hot iron and inks to make the marks.

Some Christians in their argument in support of tattooing use the writings in the book of Ezekiel to support their argument.

"And the Lord said unto him, go through the midst of the city, through the midst of Jerusalem, and set a mark upon the foreheads of the men that sign and that cry for all the abominations that be done in the midst thereof" (Ezekiel 9:4).

In this Bible passage, the Lord commanded that the righteous be marked. There is no detailed information on what object was used to mark the righteous, nevertheless, the purpose of the marking was righteous because it was orchestrated by God. That is not a valid reason to endorse the practice and act of tattooing by Christians. God is sovereign and He chooses whatever method that suits Him to carry out His divine purpose at any time. For example in the gospels, Jesus healed using various methods; He laid hands on the sick, He spoke the word, and it was once recorded that He spat on the mud and healed a blind man (John 9:6), that does not mean it is a practice that should be adopted. We do not go about spitting on muds to heal or cure blindness today, therefore, we do not assume that the occurrence in Ezekiel 9:4 is a justification for tattooing today.

Another Scriptural reference some Christians use to justify tattooing is found in Revelation 19:16,

"And He had on His vesture and on His thigh a name written, King of kings and Lord of lords."

The Christians who use this as an argument in support of tattooing, believing that at the Second Coming of Jesus, He will have a tattoo on His thigh. It is amazing that some Christians could believe that. Can anyone with the spirit of discernment who is also filled with the Holy Spirit believe that at all? I believe they say such things only to justify themselves of the evil activity. They do not know that by saying this (that Jesus had tattoo on His thigh) what they mean is that:

1. Jesus was a sinner

2. Jesus was defiled and unholy

3. Jesus was not the sinless, spotless lamb of God

But the Bible makes us know that in Jesus there is no sin.

1 John 3:5 says:

"And ye know that he was manifested to take away our sins; and in him is no sin."

Knowing that our bodies are the temple of God, tattooing is one of the ways of defiling it. As said earlier, we have different kinds of purity and physical purity is against the idea of tattooing as rejected by God himself.

1 Corinthians 3:16-17.

"Know ye not that ye are the temple of God, and that the Spirit of God dwelleth in you? If any man defile the temple of God, him shall God destroy, for the temple of God is holy which temple ye are."

Jesus Christ is not pleased with any Christian wearing a pagan or idol picture on his body. This is because such a practice has its root in paganism and idol worship. Remember God said that, whosoever defiles the temple of God, him will He destroy.

My heart bleeds when I see people defiling the temple with the excuse that others are doing so. And they refuse to see the consequences.

Numbers 23:19 says:

"God is not a man that he should lie, neither the son of man, that he should repent; hath he said and shall not do it or hath he spoken, and shall he not make It good."

Therefore, do not be deceived in any way, for God cannot be mocked and His standard cannot change because of you and I.

Leviticus 19:27 states the mind of God. He saw that cutting of hair and beard became a common idolatrous practice in Egypt, Canaan, Arabia and some other neighboring countries and signifies dedication to idols and glorifying idols more than God. In those days, many people were very violent, both in mourning and worshiping of idol. They cut their hair and their God-given flesh because of their superstitious belief. This was an insult to God and it made Him to forbid any cutting on the flesh.

Chapter 2

THE VICES OF TATTOOING

1. IT CAN BE A SOURCE OF DEADLY COMMUNICABLE DISEASES

This seemingly harmless drawing on your body can ruin your entire life. It is a means of acquiring deadly diseases such as HIV, Hepatitis B, Tetanus, Syphilis, and skin diseases. Some researchers say that tattooing may be the number one distributor of Hepatitis C because of the number people, who troop into tattoo shops to acquire this deadly mark.

It has also been said that hepatitis B can be transmitted through drawing made with contaminated needles and tattoo machines. I begin to wonder what anyone would tell his creator when he dies as a result of these diseases, all in the name of acquiring an evil mark (tattoo). And it will also interest you to know that after getting tattooed, the American Red Cross prohibits you from donating blood until after one year of the tattoo.

Besides, tattooing can cause skin diseases such as sarcoid, keloid, scaring allergic dermatitis and tumors. Also a lot of people react to the tattoo inks. Tattoo can cause harm to your exposed flesh through the ink and marks and in some cases can cause serious sore.

Psalm 38:5-8 says:

My wounds stink and are corrupt because of my foolishness.

I am troubled; I am bowed down greatly; I go mourning all the day long.

For my loins are filled with a loathsome disease and there is no soundness in my flesh.

I am feeble and sore broken: I have roared by reason of the disquietness of my heart.

2. IT IS A MARK OF REBELLION

The act of rebellion is highly despised by God. Rebellion led to the destruction of many kingdoms in the Bible. The Scripture equates the act of rebellion to witchcraft which was an offense punishable by stoning to death.

"For rebellion is as a sin of witchcraft" (1 Samuel 15:23).

"Thou shall not suffer a witch to live." (Exodus 22:18)

There is nothing good about tattoo. Rather it shows the world how rebellious you are. In some societies, tattoo is associated with prostitutes and street boys.

It is a mark of rebellion, and shows that one has stepped beyond the norms and values of the society. Having tattoo could make an individual look irresponsible or judged as such by people around. Some professional organizations will not hire a person with tattoos in a visible part of the body because it is considered as unprofessional.

It amazes me to see young ladies these days

exposing their breasts just for people to notice their tattoos. Some people wear tattoos as a mark of social acceptance into certain circles and also to make a statement to people.

The Latin word for tattoo is "stigma" it is a mark of disgrace and reproach. In those days, tattoo was drawn in the body of slaves to differentiate them or on the body of prisoners to know those who committed serious crimes. Apart from being a mark of rebellion, it is an act of indecency and depravity.

In some countries, one of the ways of rehabilitating prisoners is the removal of the tattoos on their bodies, which they believe contribute to their criminal behavior.

It is also believed that people with tattoo are stubborn and suicidal at any time. Why? Because of the rebellious spirit associated with the mark they are bearing on their bodies. Father Greg Boyle in 1988 started a program (Homeboys Industries) in East Los Angeles to help ex-gang members free tattoo removals to help them find a job and some to turn their lives around.

Having a tattoo with the sign of a snake can

open the door to serpentine spirits and other demonic oppression. As Christians, we are to "walk circumspectly and wisely and also to redeem the time because the days are evil (Ephesians 5:15-16). Because we are spirit beings, we need to cultivate the habit of walking in the spirit and be discerning. There are many seducing spirits in the world that are luring people away from the faith.

"Now the Spirit speaketh expressly, that in the latter times some shall depart from the faith, giving heed to seducing spirits, and doctrines of devils" (1 Timothy 4:1 KJV).

Christians are to be watchful and vigilant and understand that these are perilous times and should be mindful of how they live. Every thought should be brought to the obedience of Christ and the heart should be guarded diligently.

Besides, tattoo is always linked with deviant behaviors and should not be seen in the lives of Christians. 'A study by researchers at Texas Tech University found a link between the number of more tattoos a person has and the amount of "deviance" they were involved in. But that isn't the whole story.

A survey of close to 2,000 college students by a group of researchers known as the "Body Art Team" found that people who have four or more tattoos are more likely to report the regular use of marijuana, the occasional use of other illegal drugs and a history of being arrested. To a lesser degree, they were also more likely to binge drink, cheat on college work and be sexually promiscuous"

Most people say that Jesus was a rebel, but beloved, He was never rebellious, but a revolutionary leader. Although He was seen to have been in opposition against the laid down tradition and principles which were in contradiction to the meaning and purpose of the Kingdom, He was constantly in obedience to His Heavenly Father, even unto death.

Philippian 2:8 says:

"And being found in fashion as a man, he humbled himself, and became obedient unto death, even the death of the cross."

Even when Christ knew he was going to die, he never rebelled against the will of the Father, but continued praying for His Father's will to be done. He said, "Father, if thou be willing, remove this cup from me: Nevertheless not my will, but thou be done" (Luke 22:42).

3. IT IS A SYMBOL OF SATAN (DEATH)

Jesus called Satan death in the book of Revelation Chapter 6. This means that if you have tattoo on your body, you have the mark of death and the spirit of death will automatically be assigned to you.

Revelation 6: 8 says:

"And I looked, and behold a pale horse: and his name that sat on him was death and hell followed with him. And power was given unto them over the fourth part of the earth, to kill with sword, and with hunger and with death, and with the beasts of the earth."

Man was created to live forever, but sin led to the Fall of Man which caused man to be expelled from the Garden of Eden, leading to spiritual death and separation from God.

1 John 5:12 says: says,

"He that hath the son has life, and he that hath not the son of God hath not life."

This means that it is either you are for God or against Him. You cannot have tattoo on your body and be speaking in tongues. Of course you could speak for Satan.

With reference to the above Bible passages ,one would see that, tattoo brings strange fire. So, there will be strange fire burning in the life of a person who has tattoo on his body. This fire could bring sickness, hatred, rejection, bad luck and other bad things. Some people complain of hotness of the body, but have they sat down to check the mystery of the tattoo or mark on their bodies, which should be seriously dealt with?

Furthermore, tattoo is a mark of Satan to torture mankind

Mark 5:1-5 says

"And they came over unto the other side of the sea, into the country of the Gadarenes.And when he was come out of the ship, immediately there met him, out of the tombs a man with an unclean spirit. Who had his dwelling among the tombs and no man could bind him, no, not with chains. Because that he had been often bound with fetters and chains, and the chains had been plucked asunder by him, and the fetters broken into

pieces: neither could any man tame him. And always, night and day, he was in the mountains and in the tombs, crying and cutting himself with stone."

This was part of the beginning of tattoo. The Bible made us to know that the devil came to steal, to kill and to destroy. Tattoo is one of the ways the devil uses to torture people, even though he has sneaked in, in the name of fashion. Immediately you put on this devil's mark on your body, you become his candidate and remember that Bible calls Satan "the great dragon" therefore, you automatically have on your body the mark of the serpent.

Revelation 12:9 says:

"And the great dragon was cast out, that old serpent, called the devil and Satan which deceiveth the whole world: he was cast out into the earth, and his angels were cast out with him."

4. IT IS A SATANIC CULTURE

From the outset tattoo has been a pagan and idol worship sign and belief. It was never rooted in Christianity. It is a practice adopted by lukewarm Christians. It has always been rooted in mysticism, cannibalism and madness as seen in the book of (Mark 5:1-5)

No matter how you try to justify this satanic mark, tattoo came from occult practices used for astral projection into the spiritual world. Most people are actually ignorant of this but thank God, you are reading this book today, so, desist from it, if you take pleasure in it. It is satanic and mystic but those who know this will not tell you since you are not part of them. In some cultures, especially in the Middle East and Arabian countries, is a cultural rite to initiate you into certain stages in their idol worship. Some people have a particular mark, which differentiates them from others. Tattoo is more than just a body decoration, it is demonic.

A friend of mine, who had a tattoo noticed that whenever she used the anointing oil on her body, the tattoo spot would be itching her seriously. This continued for a long time until she went for deliverance and God delivered her from it. Satan is the chief thief and he has come to destroy mankind; therefore, Tattoo is one of his weapons. Tattoo originated from practice of magic, whereby they call the spirit of a person in or out of the person. In the eastern part of Nigeria, if somebody has a serious headache, he will be taken to a herbalist, who will make a tattoo on his forehead to tame the spirit responsible.

This they do, thereby making the body of the person a permanent abode for the evil spirit, which they tame and it will not trouble the person externally anymore.

Hosea 4:6 says:

"My people are destroyed for lack of knowledge: because thou hast rejected knowledge, I will also reject thee, that thou shall be no priest to me: seeing thou hast forgotten the law of thy God, I will also forget thy children."

The numerous piercing of the skin gives demons access to the body with the help of their inks. The inks sometime are not ordinary; most of them have passed through some ritual screening to help them gain access into the astral world .

For instance, in the Eastern part of Nigeria, when a person dies in an accident, it is believed that the person will come back again (reincarnation). In that case, a tattoo is drawn on the body of the person to identify him or her in the next incarnation. Also, when a woman has a stillbirth, the baby is given a similar mark, so that if it is a spirit, the baby will not come back again to torment the parents.

In Hinduism, it is believed that without tattoo, parents will not be able to recognize their children in the next world. And some believe that wearing tattoo would make them acquire strength and to get a place in heaven. Also, in some cultures, they believe that tattoo is meant for protection against gunshot, to cure certain illness, beautify the body, for attraction, to get spiritual strength and to gain survival of soul after death. Some believe that putting it on their foreheads would attract good luck and protection against witchcraft. Therefore, one could see that tattoo is a satanic rite, which involves sacrifice and blood covenant connected with religious practices to put human souls in bondage.

According to some missionaries, whenever any pagan is converted to Christ, the first thing they do is to remove his tattoo, knowing that it is an instrument of Satan.

5. IT IS AN OCCULT SOURCE OF POWER

Tattoo is one of the ways of blood-letting which releases demonic powers as life is in the blood. The occult world believes so much in blood, because it is a source of power to them. This is why they always carry out human sacrifice as a source of their satanic strength.

According to some religions, it is believed that blood-letting releases power to the occult world. Therefore, tattooists may be performing rituals during their tattoo making, which may be unknown to the person wearing the tattoo. Tattooing is also associated with Baal worshippers as recorded in 2 Kings 18:28:

"And they cried aloud and cut themselves after their manner with knives and lancets, till the blood gushed out upon them."

Remember, the Bible says they make the tattoo, "after their manner", which means, the Baal worshippers are known for this, which they believe is a source of power. To acquire this demonic power, most occult men do not mind walking naked in the cemetery at night or cutting themselves for bloodletting.

Any activity that involves bloodletting is satanic and since tattoo is a bloodletting activity, it is a satanic practice.

It pains my heart when I see young ladies exposing these satanic marks without knowing that they have been initiated into occultism. Some of the inks they rub on the wound are not ordinary inks but concoctions prepared by witch doctors which they use to initiate innocent people who patronize them.

I heard the story of a certain man, who wanted a tattooist to tattoo his manhood; I wonder why he wanted it there. We are in a wicked world; he probably wanted it there to initiate people. And anyone who eventually has sex with him may be initiated. Occult people devised various means of getting souls into the kingdom of darkness.

John 10:10 says;

"The thief cometh not, but for to steal, and to kill; and to destroy; I am come that they might have life and that they might have it more abundantly."

Any woman who jumps from one man to another will have many powers to contend with because most of these men deliberately put on tattoo not as fashion but to steal people's virtues, thereby depositing poisons into the bodies of their victims. In future, such ladies complain of moving objects in their bodies. All these are tactics of the enemy for the end time.

6. IT IS A MARK OF SHAME

Tattoo is one of the ways the enemy uses to cage the souls of men and to subject them to self-pity. If you go closer to some of the people who have these marks and they open up to you, you will pity them. Most of them will actually tell you that they want it removed.

Laura Reybold, one of the tattoo authors said, "An ever rising number of people are so unhappy with their tattoo, that they are willing to pay anything to have them removed."

Tattoo has made a lot of people to lose good things in life. For example, some employers of labor do not employ people with tattoos in their bodies; they look at them as irresponsible people. And when such people lose such opportunities, they begin to pity themselves.

It is time the truth be told; no responsible man will want to marry a lady with tattoo and vice versa because our society sees this as a mark of indecency and a taboo.

Tattoo is like a cloth you put on and you will not be able to walk freely on the street, because as you are walking, people are looking at you strangely. Sometime ago, in a nearby supermarket, a lady with a tattoo wanted to help a baby and the mother of the baby just screamed that she should not touch her baby with that hand.

Recently I met a lady who told me that she lost a good opportunity because of her tattoo, she went for an interview and she was not allowed in because the organization does not take people with tattoo.

So, what is the gain in it when after making the expensive and painful tattoo, you start looking for a way to get rid of it? The emotional and social torture is too much that if care is not taken, you lose good friends, as no parents would want to see their children with people bearing tattoo. It is time for us to be wise and realize the tactics of the enemy to take away good things from us.

Sometime ago a friend of mine told me the genesis of her mother's troubled marriage. She said her parents were best of friends until the father came back from work one day to meet her mother with tattoo, which her friends convinced her to do, as part of the reigning fashion of the day. She said beginning from that day, her father hated her mother till death. This caused a lot of trouble that even when the man died, his brothers collected everything from the woman, as they believed that she killed their brother. When the woman acquired this mark, the devil crept in and the man developed a serious sickness till death. This is the way Satan uses to waste good things. Seeing that the family was happy, he convinced the woman to go for tattoo, which her husband did not like. I pray that the devil will not take away your joy, in Jesus' name. Amen.

Many people will never tell you what they are passing through since they put this mark of Satan on their bodies but spiritually and physically, their dream lives have become a battlefield and many of them are running from pillar to post, looking for solution.

1 Thessalonians 5:22-23;

"Abstain from all appearance of evil. And the very God of peace sanctify you wholly; and I pray God your whole spirit and soul and body be preserved blameless unto the coming of our Lord Jesus Christ."

Chapter 3

THE WAY OUT

Since the devil has used this evil mark to capture many young people in the Body of Christ, it is now the responsibility of the church not to condemn them but to bring them back to God and to destroy the effect of these satanic marks. Knowing that tattooing also crept into the church through Christian rock music, believers must desist from listening to them. Many believers deceive themselves by drawing the mark of the cross on their bodies forgetting that God cannot be mocked.

2 Corinthians 2:11

"Lest Satan should get advantage of us: for we are not ignorant of his devices."

God prohibits tattoo and that ends it. Lying to justify yourself with what you call a Christian mark is a sign that you are on a journey to Hell fire. God does not want tattoo and that settles it. The solution is not for those, who intend to get the marks, but for those who have realized their mistakes and want to go back to God.

1. **ACKNOWLEDGE YOUR SIN**: Once you realize that tattoo is a sign of the devil which defiles the temple of God, (your body) you have taken a bold step already to come out of the camp of the enemy. So, once you know the truth, come to God in repentance and ask Him to forgive you. Recognize the type of mark you have, either a flower, cross or serpent. Next, try and interpret the spiritual meaning of the mark and move to the next level.

2. **GET RID OF IT**: This is not talking of the physical removal alone but also the spiritual. To do this, you have to go for deliverance or into serious prayers to cancel the effect of the tattoo in your life. The physical removal is also necessary, if it is possible. According to a 2006 survey in the Journal of the American Academy of Dermatology, 24 percent of 18 to 50-year-olds have tattoos, and 17 percent have

considered tattoo removal. In decades past, people trying to get rid of tattoos have gone to extreme measures to de-ink. For example, one technique known as dermabrasion involves scraping away or sanding down the skin. In salabrasion, a salt solution is rubbed into the skin and heated and scraped away. In both cases, when the area heals, the tattoo may be gone, but scars are likely to be left behind. Surgically removing the tattoo is also likely to leave a scar. The tattooed skin is cut out and the surrounding skin is sewn back together. Occasionally, doctors can perform surgical removals of tiny tattoos.

Besides, the most important aspect of it is to get rid of the spiritual effects which are:

- Mark of indecency

- Mark of shame and defilement

- Mark of satanic culture

- Mark of initiation

To do this, lay your hands on the mark and pray it out of your life and destiny. Since you know that some of these marks open doors for demons, pray that any evil that entered your life as a result of the evil mark should come out and die. Pray until you are convinced in your spirit that you are free.

3. **FORGIVE YOURSELF**: Knowing that tattoo is a taboo that God and the society dislike, you have to forgive yourself for ever putting it on. Forget it and move on, there is nothing God cannot do. I heard the testimony of a sister, who got born again at a crusade and the following day, the taboo on her body disappeared. This is a true-life story. So, even if it did not disappear physically in your own case, the spiritual disappearance matters most. So, forgive yourself and move on with your life.

"Jesus said unto her, I am the resurrection, and the life; he that believeth in me though he were dead, yet shall he live" John 11:25.

"Forasmuch then as the children are partakers of flesh and blood, he [Jesus] also himself likewise took part of the same; that through death he might destroy him that had the power of death, that is the devil" Hebrews 2:14.

All scriptures in the foregoing show that it is

only Christ that has the power to destroy the works of Satan. Therefore, once you accept that Christ died for you and you confess Jesus as your personal Saviour, the Blood of Christ has the power to remove every mark of death from your life.

Since tattoo is a curse, stay away from it. Tattoo is one of the fastest ways the devil is using to cage the souls of men, in this last hour. So, be wise and be heavenly minded.

4. **REMOVE AND REVOKE IT**: Tattoo has gotten many into unconscious initiation. So, once you reject this mark, the next thing is to revoke any covenant and oath that took place as a result of this mark. Reject the membership and cling to Jesus, who is the author and finisher of our faith. The power of God will redeem you from the curse attached to it and set you free.

"Christ has redeemed us from the curse of the law being made a curse for us for cursed is any one that hangeth on a tree" Galatians 3:13.

Finally, give no place to the devil and be wise as serpent as the word of God warms.

"Neither give place to the devil" Ephesians 4:27.

Dear reader I pray that if you already have this mark and you want God's intervention, the God of Elijah will arise and have mercy upon you and deliver you, in Jesus' name. Amen.

BIBLE QUOTATIONS

"In him was life: and the life was the light of men" (John 1:4).

"For the wages of sin is death; but the gift of God is eternal life through Jesus Christ our Lord" (Romans 6:23).

"Forasmuch as ye know that ye were not redeemed with corruptible things as silver and gold, for your vain conversation received by tradition from your fathers. But with the precious blood of Christ, as for a lamb without blemish and without spot" (1 Peter 1:18-19).

PRAYER POINTS

1. Oh Lord! Arise and have mercy upon me in Jesus name.

2. Blood of Jesus cleanse my body, soul and spirit.

3. I purge my spirit soul and body with the blood of Jesus.

4. Any evil present in my body as a result of tattoo, your time is up, die.

5. Powers tormenting me as a result of any mark on my body, die in Jesus name.

6. Any door I have opened to Satan in my life, I close it in Jesus name,

7. Oh God! Arise and show me mercy in Jesus name.

8. You my body receive total deliverance in Jesus name.

PART 2

PURITY

Brethren, it is high time we know our stand in the Lord, as most of us have completely forgotten the most important things He wants from us and we are busy chasing shadows. It is time for us to know that holiness is a requirement in our walk with God.

"Follow peace with all men and holiness, without which no man shall see the Lord" (Hebrew 12:14).

The Bible does not say without money, beauty or any other thing you might have, but without holiness no one can see God. Therefore, to see God and to lay hold of His promises for us, we need to purify our spirits, souls and bodies according to God's standard of righteousness.

"Blessed are the pure in heart: for they shall see God" (Matthew 5:8).

We are in the last days and, today most churches are filled with mixed multitudes who only seek to minister to their carnal needs and are not too interested in their spiritual growth or becoming disciples of Jesus. Many young people are carried away by worldly standards of Hollywood and have been deceived and ensnared by the wayward lifestyles of the celebrities. Holiness or purity according to them is obsolete and boring; but God's standards do not change. These things ought not to be.

And Luke 12:31 says:

"Seek ye first the kingdom of God and his righteousness and every other thing shall be added unto you."

Purity is the bedrock of miracles. The passage above says, except you are pure in heart, you cannot see God. It will be a great tragedy for you to come to this wicked world, receive all the miracles and at the end miss heaven. We need to ask the Holy Spirit to put His flood light through us and search us and purge us of any form of ungodliness.

"Teach me thy way, O LORD; I will walk in thy truth: unite my heart to fear thy name" (Psalms 86:11).

My prayer is that the Holy Spirit will use the writings of this book to help you find your way back to the Lord and live a life pleasing to the Master. God bless you as you do so.

Chapter 1

WHAT IS PURITY?

Purity can be defined as the absence of spiritual, moral and physical defilement.

It is the godly standard of holiness and cleanliness of the spirit, soul and body. The emphasis is on the "spirit, soul and body" and not just the outward appearance, but the whole person. Filthiness, shabby and an unkempt appearance do not depict holiness.

Purity can also be described as total separation from worldliness and everything that does not glorify God.

It is a state of being upright, clean, complete and morally good in all ramifications and without evil thoughts or actions. It is shunning wicked lifestyles and worldliness.

Titus 2:14 says:

"Who gave himself for us that he might redeem us from all iniquity, and purify unto himself a peculiar people, zealous of good works."

The book of Titus shows a very good example of God's mind towards mankind; the State of Man, The Doom of Sinners, and, the Doctrine of Holiness. According to the Dakes Bible "The Bible is true, read it and be wise, believe it and be holy and safe." It is only when you are holy that you can be safe.

There are levels you cannot reach spiritually if you're not following God's standard of purity. When you are unclean, the Holy Spirit cannot dwell in you and there would be room for other powers to come in.

For example, it is true that God is always ready to forgive us our sins, but contrary to the belief of many, we are not to continue in our sins. God is a merciful Father and He will always forgive us once we run to Him, nevertheless, we should not take His grace for granted. Look at what the Bible says in

Romans 6:1-2:

"What shall we say then? Shall we continue in sin, that grace may abound? God forbid. How shall we, that are dead to sin, live any longer therein."

One fact you must note is that although God forgives our sins, we cannot escape some of the consequences of sin. A pregnancy that occurs as a result of premarital sex or teenage pregnancy will have the child to always serve as a reminder of the sexual sin committed in the secret. God may have forgiven you for the sin but you are now saddled with the responsibility of raising a child you are not ready for. Although children are a blessing and will always be a blessing. Every life is precious to God but it is important to do the right thing at the right time. Even if you try and cover your sins, the devil who is the accuser of the brethren knows how to bring an accusation against the people of God.

He who covers his sins will not prosper, but whosoever confesses and forsakes them will have mercy" (Proverbs 28:13). You may think you are smart by committing secret sins, but I tell you: you cannot be smarter than the devil. He knows your spiritual level and can record your daily activities through the stars, sun, moon, air, the earth, the heavenlies and the other elements. Christians need to be wise by abstaining from every form of sin.

Most people are interested only in the promises of God; but are not willing to follow His instructions.

Obadiah 1: 17 says:

"But upon mount Zion shall be deliverance, and there shall be holiness; and the house of Jacob shall possess their possessions."

Here, God says there shall be deliverance; and the Word of God abides forever. After deliverance, holiness follows; that is, you keep yourself pure by abstaining from sin and be clean before God. When you are obedient to these instructions, God will bless you.

These days, many people pursue deliverance and the blessings attached to it. They are not interested in holiness, which is a doorway for the reward of their deliverance to come in. God is all knowing and all wise. His standards will not be changed to suit any man.

"Forever, O LORD, thy word is settled in heaven" *(Psalms 119:89).*

Many people come for deliverance but are not ready to keep God's rules and regulations. Even after their deliverance, some still continue in sinful acts and expect the blessings of God upon their lives. God cannot be mocked; a person will always reap what he sows. If you sow righteousness, you will reap the rewards of righteousness, if you sow iniquity, you will reap the rewards of iniquity.

Purity is an enabler of the blessing. You may be enjoying the good things of life but *"The blessing of the LORD makes one rich, and He adds no sorrow with it"* *(Proverbs 10:22).*

The blessing that comes from the Lord includes salvation, wholeness and peace. There is no peace for the wicked (Isaiah 48:22). The Scripture calls anyone that sins willfully a wicked person and classifies all forms of immorality as wickedness. In Genesis when interceding for Sodom, Abraham asked God not to destroy the righteous with the wicked, (Genesis 18:23).

Sometime ago, I met a sister who was

contemplating leaving the church because, according to her, the church does not permit her to dress the way she wanted. I got to know that the lady's main motive for attending church was to find a husband and continue with her way of life without any form of transformation or genuine repentance. She might be deceiving herself and others, but God cannot be mocked; He is an all-knowing God, and nothing is hidden from Him.

Galatians 6:7says:

"Be not deceived; God is not mocked for whatsoever a man soweth, that shall he also reap."

PRAYER POINTS

1. Oh Lord, by Your mercy, deliver me from my ignorance.

2. Oh God, deliver me from myself, in Jesus' name.

3. Oh Lord my father, help me to be pure before you in the name of Jesus.

Chapter 2

CLASSIFICATION OF PURITY

Purity can be classified into three major parts:

- Physical purity.

- Moral purity.

- Spiritual purity.

PHYSICAL PURITY

This is the outward purification. The purity God requires is holiness within and without. My heart bleeds that the world would be setting the standard for the church and not vice-versa. We are called to be the light of the world and the salt of the earth. The church now emulates the world in fashion, music, and many other things. One can no longer differentiate a Christian from a reveler. Jesus should always be our guide and standard for living. Shabby and unkempt look does not glorify God neither does it signify an act of humility, rather it is ignorance and a sign of slothfulness.

As Christians, we need to be clean, modest and presentable at all times. As kingdom ambassadors, we ought to represent Jesus Christ with excellence. Cleanliness is next to godliness is a very popular adage used often especially by the older generation. The Scripture admonishes us to be holy in all manner of conversation, (1 Peter 1:15). The scripture means we need to be holy in conduct and appearance; in word and in deed. The condition of the heart reflects in our actions therefore, a lustful heart will reflect in a lustful appearance.

In her testimony one day a sister said she liked dressing shabbily, because of her spiritual level; by which she meant that as a spiritual sister, putting on beautiful clothes was an act of unbrokenness. Anyway, the pastor quickly rebuked her and told her that shabby dressing was not a sign of holiness.

Our God is a God of order, splendor, beauty and glory. There is no one like Him, and no one is equal to Him in glory, power, honor and splendor. King Solomon got this revelation and built a tabernacle that could be compared to none. The tabernacle was glorious and magnificent in honor of God.

1 kings 6:20-23 says:

"And the oracle in the forepath was twenty cubits in length and twenty cubits in breadth, and the twenty cubits in the height thereof: and he over laid it with pure gold and so covered the altar which was of cedar. Solomon over laid the house within with pure gold and he made a partition by the chains of gold before the oracle and he over laid it with gold. And the whole house he overlaid with gold until he had finished the entire house: also, the whole altar that was by the oracle he overlaid with gold. And within the oracle, two cherubim of olive tree, each ten cubits high."

Note that the Bible says that we are made in the image and likeness of God; therefore, we should be like our Father. I am not saying that you are not clean, until you put on extravagant and expensive dresses or suit sewed in London or Paris; but the little you have, should be kept clean. In the Bible God told the Israelites to wash their clothes, because He does not dwell in a dirty place.

Exodus 19:10 says:

"And the Lord said unto Moses, go unto the people and sanctify them today and tomorrow, and let them wash their cloth."

Some believers do not bother to take their bath, especially during fasting. This is a wrong perception. God is a clean God. In the book of Exodus, after the sacrifice in the tabernacle, the priest had to wash his hands in the laver of brass.

Exodus 30:17-21 says:

"And the Lord spake to Moses saying; thou shalt also make a laver of brass; and his foot also of brass, to wash withal; and thou shall put it between the tabernacle of the congregation and the altar, and thou shalt put water there in. for Aaron and his son shall wash their hands and their feet thereat: so they shall wash their hands and their fret, that they die not, and it shall be a statute forever to them, even to him and to his seed throughout their generations."

The laver of brass was the second furniture in the Tabernacle courtyard. It was between the brazen altar of the burnt offering and the sanctuary. It was filled with water and the priests had to wash their hands and feet before entering the Sanctuary. Water here symbolizes the purifying action of the word of God on a person. With this reference to the word of God, a believer should be clean within and without. This is a sign of purification. Dirt will only bring harm to your life.

A closer look at what is happening in our environment will show you that even the occultic and fetish men are changing their code of conduct and modes of dressing.

For instance, the herbalists, shamans and native doctors are rebranding themselves and are up to date in their Fashion sense, appearances and live in clean and decent environments. Their era of living in slums and run-down environment is over. They now repackage their fetish materials and products, making it appealing and attractive to the buyers.

I knew a fetish man who used to appear on the television show in the African flowing attire worn by men, adorned with cowries and would chant demonic incantations. Because his appearance was somewhat scary and unattractive, he went back and repackaged himself and his products became one of the bestselling products in the market. Some demonic products have been repackaged and made attractive because appearances do matter, and good appearances do attract favor. Since appearances can be deceptive, therefore discernment is needed.

Sometime ago, a brother and I went on a street evangelism. When we got to a shop, we shared the word of God about salvation and later about prosperity. The brother quoted Philippians 4:19 which says:

"But my God shall supply all your need according to his riches in glory by Christ Jesus."

Immediately this brother quoted this verse, the eldest man in our audience lifted up his eye towards him and said, "Brother, you need that verse more than us." That was when I realized that the brother wore outdated cloths and was looking haggard and unkempt. I had to quickly intervene, and we left the place.

People are not ready to read the Bible anymore; we (believers) are the Bibles they are now reading. What you show them is what they emulate. We are the salt of the earth and the light of the world (Matthew 5:13-14).

I remember a close relation of mine, who left his church, because the pastor of the church would not dress well. He said, "Even, with an expensive suit, the man still looks untidy." He left the church saying that the pastor had nothing to offer. This means that he was looking up to the man of God. He did not bother to read his Bible to know that we are to look unto Jesus, "the author and finisher of our faith." This is simply telling us that the world will read you first before reading their Bibles. Let us be worthy examples of God's kingdom in words and in deed, because we are the light of the world.

Genesis 35:2-4 says:

"Then Jacob said unto his household and all that were with him, put away the strange gods that are among you and be clean, and change your garment.

And they gave unto Jacob all the strange gods which were in their hand and all their earrings which were in their ears; and Jacob heeds them under the oak which was by she-chem. And they journeyed: and the terror of God was upon the cities that were round about them, and they did not pursue after the son of Jacob."

For God to reveal Himself to us there are certain things we have to do away with. In most of our churches these days some sisters dress provocatively in attires that do not depict a child of God. The fashion industry has been highly sexualized, and many want to fit into the mold. Paul admonishes the church not to be conformed to the world but to be transformed by the renewing of the mind (Romans 12:2). Modesty in dressing and good Christian conduct are fast disappearing.

God's standard cannot be changed due to modernization. He remains God and His eyes cannot behold iniquity.

Finally, our outward appearance matters a lot to God and what we wear and what we do should be in agreement with His word.

MORAL PURITY

This means uprightness of character; integrity, trust worthiness and forthrightness.

2 Corinthians 6:14-15 says:

"Be ye not equally yoked together with unbelievers for what fellowship hath righteousness with unrighteousness and what communion has light with darkness. And what concord hath Christ with Beliah? Or what part hath he that believeth with an infidel?"

Here God is warning us to be separated from anything that is ungodly. We should separate ourselves from the ungodliness of the world, and be pure before God. *"We are in the world and not of the world (John 17:16).* Many believers are competing with the people of the world in order to be admired and approved of by the world. This has led many of our Christian sisters into sin. God has no room for lukewarm Christians; you cannot be on the fence or indecisive about your relationship with God. Jesus said to the Church in Laodicea,

"I know thy works, that thou art neither cold nor hot: I would thou wert cold or hot. So then because thou art lukewarm, and neither cold nor hot, I will spue thee out of my mouth" (Revelation 3:15-16).

Your lifestyle should reflect who you profess to be. People should look at you and know which kingdom you belong.

"For we are unto God a sweet savor of Christ, in them that are saved, and in them that perish: To the one we are the savor of death unto death; and to the other the savor of life unto life. And who is sufficient for these things?" (2 Corinthians 2:15-16).

That you go to church does not mean you are a child of God. All He wants from you and I is complete obedience to His will and purpose.

Sometime ago, I met a Christian brother quarreling with another person in the full glare of onlookers. When he saw the way people were amazed at his behavior, he told the person he was having issues with: "I will slap you physically and spiritually. I am violent in the Lord and I don't take rubbish from Satan." I laughed and shook my head in amazement, because we all knew he was only trying to defend himself. The truth was he had already shown his true character to everyone watching him.

Your character matters to God. He is looking out for representatives on earth and when we derail from His way, it breaks His heart. As a child of God let your walk, your stand and your speech be a reflection of Him.

Proverbs 2:20 says:

"That thou mayest walk in the way of good men, and keep the part of the righteous."

The above verse points to our behavior before God and men. May I ask you some questions: "Are people rejecting Jesus because of you?" "Does your secret life reflect the Jesus you preach in the open?" "Is God pleased with you or do you cause His heart to bleed?" If your answer to any of these questions is 'yes' then your salvation is questionable. You have serious work to do on your spiritual life. You need to search yourself, see where you have fallen short of God's expectation of you, and find your way back to the feet of the Cross.

Several years ago, in my former church, seats were reserved for the elderly, mothers, children and others. Then an evangelical team which was new to the church observed that a particular elderly man would bring cola-nut to the church and share among his fellow elders who will be chewing while the Sunday worship service was going on. If by the time they finished chewing the kola-nut and the pastor was still preaching, one of them would go to the pulpit, give the minister a sign to come down, that they were tired. This continued until they started dying one after the other. This was a very strange and evil manipulation of the service until the church rose up and prayed to God for divine intervention.

The above story shows us that people, especially servants of God, cannot come to the house of God and misbehave or do whatever they like. God is still on the throne and when He starts His punishment, no power will be able to deliver from His mighty hand. As children of God, we ought to relate to God with reverential fear and treat people with respect and honor.

It is sad to see people dishonoring God's presence and engaging in slander and gossip while the service is going on.

- What really shows that you are a child of God?

- What does your character show people around? Purity or worldliness?

- Are the words that proceed from your mouth pure or filthy?

- Does your character bring honor or reproach to the name of the Lord?

- Who are your friends? *"He that walketh with wise men shall be wise: but a companion of fools shall be destroyed" (Proverbs 13:20).*

- Remember,

Psalms 24:3-4 says:

"Who shall ascend into the hill of the Lord? Or who shall stand in his holy place? He that hath clean hands and a pure heart; who hath not lifted up his soul unto vanity, nor sworn deceitfully."

God's desire for His church is to be a house of prayer and not a den of robbers where buying and selling takes place. God desires for His children is to live a life pleasing unto Him.

The Bible says, Out of the abundance of the heart the mouth speaketh.

The way we react to things and people around us show our state of mind. Some of our brothers and sisters have what can be called "character deformation". The way they behave towards people around them or people coming into the church for the first time is so bad, that people wonder if they are Christians. Because of this, people begin to avoid them or even leave the church for another one, where they will be well treated. Remember, on the judgment day, you will give account of all those you have driven away from God with your character. Therefore, if people around you cannot give a good testimony about you, check yourself.

VISITING UNHOLY PLACES

Another aspect of moral purity is being cautious of the places you visit as a believer. There are places that the angel of God will never enter with you.

Some of the foods are polluted, and once you eat them, you are automatically defiled and the Spirit of God cannot dwell in you.

Purity is the key to God's heart, so let people around you see Christ in you and let your character be the type that pleases God.

SPIRITUAL PURITY

This is a godly standard of holiness and purity of the mind. It is the absence of contamination and pollution of the spirit and soul. It is the inward state of a man's heart which can only be seen by God. A song writer says:

- How about your heart?

- Is it right with God?

- Is it blackened by sin?

- Is it stained within?

- Could Christ come into it to stay?

Matthew 15:19-20 says:

"For out of the heart proceed evil thoughts, murders adulteries, fornication, thefts, false witness, blasphemies: These are the things which defile a man."

These are serious questions you need to ask yourself and faithfully answer them, because what goes on in your heart is important to God. Remember,

Matthew 5:8 says:

"Blessed are the pure in heart, for they shall see God."

What you meditate on, in your heart can either glorify God or defile you.

Proverbs 23:7 says:

"As he thinketh in his heart, so is he."

2 Corinthians 10: 5 says:

"Casting down imaginations and every high thing that exalteth itself against the knowledge of God and bringing into captivity every though to the obedience of Christ."

Brethren, it is time for you to arrest those spirits and evil thoughts that are defiling you before God. God cannot reveal His secrets to a polluted heart and the Holy Spirit cannot dwell in such a heart.

Chapter 3

WHAT THE HEART OF A CHILD OF GOD IS MEANT FOR

1. To Seek God:

Psalms 119:2 says:

"Blessed are they that keep his testimonies and that seek him with the whole heart."

2 Chronicles 15:15 says:

"And all Judah rejoiced at the oath for they had sworn with all their heart, and sought him with their whole desire and he was found of them, and the Lord gave them rest round about."

2. To Praise God:

Psalms 9:1 says:

"I will praise thee, O Lord, with my whole heart: I will shew forth all thy marvelous works."

Psalm 119:1 says:

"Blessed are the undefiled in the way, who walk in the law of the Lord."

3. To Observe the Truth:

Psalms 119:34 says:

"Give me understanding, and I shall keep thy law, yea, I shall observe it with my whole heart."

4. To Entreat God's Favor:
Psalms 119:58 says:

"I entreated thy favor with my whole heart, be merciful unto me according to thy word."

5. To Keep Commandments:
Psalms 119:69 says:

"The proud have forged a lie against me, but I will keep thy precepts with my whole heart."

Joshua 1:8 says:

"This book of the law shall not depart out of thy mouth; but thou shall meditate therein day and night, that thou mayest observe to do according to all that is written therein; for then thou shalt make thy way prosperous, and then thou shall have good success."

6. To Cry to God:
Psalms 119:145 says:

"I cried with my whole heart; hear me O Lord, I will keep thy statutes."

7. To Repent from Backsliding:

Jeremiah 24:7 says:

"I will give them a heart to know me, that I am the Lord, and they shall be my people and I will be their God: for they shall return unto me with their whole heart."

THOUGHTS THAT DEFILE THE SOUL

- General wickedness   Genesis 6:5.

- Jealousy   Genesis 50:20.

- Evading responsibility   Deuteronomy 15:9.

- False witnessing   Deuteronomy 19:15.

- False decisions   Judges 15:2.

- Murder and rape   Judges 20:5.

- False security   Psalms 49: 11.

- Worry   Luke 12: 11-2.

- Adultery   Matthew 5:32.

- Fornication   Matthew 5:32.

- Lasciviousness   Galatians 5:19.

- Pride   Luke 9:46-48.

- Cursing rulers   Ecclesiastes 10:20.

- Evil imagination   Job 21:27.

- P1otting to kill   Esther 3:6.

- False accusation   Matthew 9:3-4.

- Wanting God's power for gain   Acts 18:18-24.

- Vanity and anxiety   Jeremiah 14:14.

- Unbelief and doubt   Luke 24:38.

God is no respecter of persons. Once your heart is not clean, He will never dwell in it.

And once the devil sees that kind of heart, he will take over. That is why you need to invite God into your heart to stay permanently. Then you now begin to meditate daily on the word of God, to allow the Holy Spirit to continue to dwell richly in you, giving you access to God's mind always. That is why

Philippians 4:8 says:

Finally, brethren, whatsoever things are true, whatsoever things are honest, whatsoever things are just, whatsoever things are pure, whatsoever things are lovely, whatsoever things are of good report; if there be any virtue, and if there be any praise, think on these things.

Other sources of spiritual pollution are eating and having sex in the dream. Night caterers feed their victims in the dream, to pollute them before God. That is why some people do not have a breakthrough even after praying. They wonder why: "But I am holy in all ramifications," they would say. But the truth is that they have been polluted spiritually and this goes a long way in hindering them from the move of God in their lives.

Therefore, eating and having sex in the dream should not be taken with levity.

DREAMS TO WATCH OUT FOR

1. Being sprayed with perfume in the dream. You do not know where the perfume came from.

2. Being sprayed with feaces in the dream. It will pollute the person spiritually with the spirit of rejection.

3. Bathing with dirty water.

4. Swimming in a dirty or swampy mud in the dream.

5. Romancing or having sex in the dream, etc.

PRAYER POINTS

1. Powers polluting me day and night, die, in Jesus' name.

2. Agents of pollution attached to my life, die, in Jesus' name.

3. Oh Lord, arise and wash me with Your Word, that I may be clean.

4. Oh Lord, arise, change my heart and let it be Your dwelling place.

5. Oh God, arise, take over my life for Your glory, in Jesus' name.

Chapter 4

PURITY IN THE PLACE OF WORSHIP

There are some perplexing experiences that need to be corrected. People do certain things in the house of worship and you will wonder, if they have the fear of God in them at all. The believer is supposed to be the House of God - the temple of the Holy Spirit (1 Corinthians 3:16; 1 Corinthians 6:19).

SOME STRANGE BEHAVIORS

1. Defiling the Altar: The altar is a place of worship which must be kept holy at all times. It represents the seat of God that should be treated with respect. But the way people walk into the altar these days to do whatever they like is really appalling. In the era of the children of Israel, it was not everybody that went into the tabernacle. Even the priest must be holy before entering the Holy of Holies, if not he would not come out alive. If you do not relate to God with respect, He will not honor you, and that can be very dangerous.

In as much as we should respect the "altar", God no longer dwells in man made altars but in human altars. The Spirit-filled believer, carrying the presence of the Lord makes the altar holy and not vice-versa (Acts 7:48; Acts 17: 24; 1 Corinthians 3:16-17); Our hearts have become God's altar because that is where the Spirit of God dwells while our bodies have become the Temple of the God. Romans 12:1 calls the believer's body the "living sacrifice." Believers have become what we can call altars of sacrifice and altars of service. Altar of sacrifice-Romans 12:1; altars of service-transformation, purpose, service, intercession etc. 1 Peter 2:5 calls the Christian a living stone, a spiritual house.

2. Dressing: Looking good, they say, is good business. But in recent times, people wear anything they like to the house of God. They wear whatever seems right to them in the name of fashion. The way you dress goes a long way to show who you are and the state of your mind. It is the way you will be addressed. Most ladies now move about the streets half-naked. You see some of them, their trousers cover only half of their bottoms, and their under wears are exposed. It is a pity that most of them do not know the origin of that kind of dressing. My heart bleeds when I see some sisters wearing these demonic dresses to the house of God, in the name of fashion. Brethren, we must be wise and mindful of the things we do, because the devil has released his agents into the world to manipulate people, and it is unfortunate that many have fallen into his traps.

Beware! Satanic agents are in the church to carry out evil agenda with their mode of dressing and the irony of it is that the ignorant ones innocently join them, leading themselves into destruction.

Brethren, our God is holy. Evil dressing should not be allowed in His house. Some deceive themselves by saying, "God does not look at the outward appearance, but inward." Brethren, let us stop deceiving ourselves for

Galatians 6:7 says:

Be not deceived; God is not mocked: for whatsoever a man soweth, that shall he also reap.

Out of the abundance of the heart, the mouth speaks. The state of the heart is reflective in the way you dress and behave.

3. Empty Promises: When you come into the house of the Lord, close your mouth, listen to the word of God and believe God for your miracles, instead of making empty promises that you may not be able to fulfill.

Deuteronomy 23:21 says:

"When thou shalt vow a vow unto the Lord thy God, thou shall not slack to pay it, for the Lord thy God will surely require it of thee; and it would be sin in thee."

Most times people defile themselves before God by not paying their vows. If you do not fulfill your promises to people, it gets to a time that they will stop believing you. This also applies to the things of God.

A pastor told me a story of a brother who came to him for prayers and said, "Pastor, if I get this contract of #10 million naira, I promise to give the church #1 million. The pastor went into series of fasting and prayers and at the end the brother got the contract but thereafter he left the church and changed his phone number. However, the next time the pastor saw him, things had gone so bad for him that even his children were begging the pastor for money to eat. The pastor had to give them some money. Most people are like this, but I pray you will not be one of them in Jesus name.

4. Talkativeness in The House Of God:

Most times you wonder why some people come to church, because the only time they are not talking is when they are sleeping. Right inside the church they would be talking during the sermon, either about politics, football or some unnecessary issues. Sometimes, it could be husband and wife, who would go back to the same house, chatting away. They fail to realize it is the tactic of the enemy to steal from them. One day I left the place I was sitting in a church because of a brother who was interpreting for the pastor right on his seat. He was doing this for no other reason but to impress people and I had no option but to change my seat. Because the devil is very intelligent and if you fail to identify his tactics quickly, he will ruin your salvation. That is why we need to be very careful.

5. Murmuring: This is one of the things that God hates with perfect hatred. He punished the Israelites seriously because of the sin of murmuring. Remember that Miriam and Aaron murmured against Moses when Moses took an Ethiopian woman. This brought leprosy upon Miriam. In some churches, when the man of God mentions certain things, especially money, some people start murmuring. Brethren, if you do not have money to contribute, it is better to keep quiet than to murmur against the man of God and thereby incur the wrath of God. I believe nobody will ask you to leave the church if you do not contribute anything, instead of bringing a curse upon yourself. Remember that God reported to Moses several times that the children of Israel were murmuring against Him and Moses. This shows that murmuring is a great sin in the sight of God.

I pray that this book will turn things around for good in your life in Jesus' name, Amen.

ABOUT THE AUTHOR

Glory Oluchi Ikeora formally know in her first edition as Glory Nwakanma is a woman of God and an advocate for Christ.

She studied History and International Relations from Abia State University and did her post graduate studies in Guidance and Counselling from University of Lagos Akoka. Through her experience and some researched work as a counsellor and with the help of Holy Spirit she wrote this life changing book.

She is a mother of two and a wife to her loving husband.